"The Road Less Traveled: Being a Black Republican in America"

By

Mr. Julian L. Boykin MBA, MS, PMP, CISM

Table of Contents

Acknowledgment: I would like to thank my wife Theresa for being my biggest supporter,biggest critic, and for helping me write this book.

Thank you to my family and friends for helping me bring my idea to fruition and taking time out of your day to support me on this journey. I would also like to thank Dr. Foster Scotland for believing me, not allowing me to dwell in my darkest moment, and being the true definition of a friend.

Chapter 1: Embracing Individuality: Discovering Republicanism:

As our society becomes ever more politically divisive and complex racial dynamics evolve, embracing individualism and exploring unique ideological paths is increasingly rewarding in today's climate. Black individuals who identify as Republicans face both opportunities and challenges when taking this journey of discovery; this chapter delves deeper into this topic by investigating factors that lead to Republicanism among Black individuals and exploring why individuality matters within larger social settings.

Unveiling the Narrative:

Step one in becoming an individualistic Black Republican involves dissecting society's expectations about Black people identifying with one party over another due to historical ties or policy platforms shared among all races, yet some Black individuals find resonance with conservative principles like limited government, free markets, and individual liberties; they challenge notions that political affiliation should be predetermined based on race; instead emphasizing individual values and beliefs as keys components in making up oneself as individuals.

History of Black Republicans:

Researching the historical context of Black Republicans can uncover an expansive legacy dating back to Reconstruction-era America, including figures such as Frederick Douglass and Booker T Washington to more contemporary voices like Condoleezza Rice and Tim Scott - Black Republicans have long been part of America's political fabric; understanding their history provides both connection and motivation, further solidifying why individuality as part of being Black is both valid and significant.

Personal Journey:

Every individual's path toward Black Republicanism is unique and determined by individual experiences. Some may have grown up in conservative homes and communities while others might encounter influential mentors or have transformative encounters which led them towards acceptance of Black Republicanism. Sharing personal accounts provides a deeper understanding of individuals' diverse motivations behind adopting them while emphasizing individual agency in decision-making processes. I used to be a Democrat and I thought they had the solutions to everything, but looking back, I remember my turning point.

In 2015, I was in Huntsville, AL, I was having a conversation with Councilman Richard Showers. I raised the question about Homeownership, Entrepreneurship, and Financial Literacy for African Americans, and my questions were put on the back burner. These three core values are the foundation for African Americans closing the wealth gap when compared to other ethnicities. Out of all three core values, Financial Literacy is the most important one to me. Not being able to read has been a major setback for the African American community. Just being able to own a home, a family can use the equity to start a business. Being able to own a business will create jobs, the chance to earn unlimited income, generational wealth for your kids, and decide when you want to work.

Submit to Criticism and Challenges:

Accepting one's individuality as a Black Republican does not come without its difficulties, however. Skepticism from both within the Black community and from within the Republican Party itself may arise from time to time; some individuals may question why one would support an institution that has often struggled to ensure racial inclusivity while others could view their affiliation with it as betraying collective identity or abandoning collective pride altogether. Navigating these obstacles requires resilience, self-reflection, dialogue, and understanding at every opportunity possible.

Identity and Intersectionality:

Being a Black Republican means navigating the complex intersectionality between race, politics, personal identity, and individualism. Recognizing racial disparities while adhering to conservative principles poses unique challenges; Black Republicans frequently work within their party to raise awareness while simultaneously pushing conservative solutions - creating an insightful understanding both individually and of how these fit within larger social environments.

Conclusion:

Being an individualist as a Black Republican requires ongoing self-exploration, growth, and engagement with society at large. Donning one's individualism within this larger political landscape allows Black Republicans to add their unique ideologies that shape conversations, policies, and American democracy itself.

CHAPTER 2: Ancestral Influences: The Legacy of Black Republicans in History

Introduction:

The legacy of Black Republicans in American history stands as evidence of their significant contributions to the Republican Party. In this chapter, we investigate ancestral influences on their formation while also looking back into history to gain a fuller appreciation of what role these figures, movements, and events play in shaping political dialogue as advocates for change.

Historical Pioneers:

To fully appreciate the legacy of Black Republicans, one must go back to the Reconstruction period following Civil War. Notable figures such as

Frederick Douglass - an influential abolitionist and social reformer-and Hiram Revels (the first African American U.S. senator) emerged as trailblazers by challenging social norms while championing civil rights within the Republican Party; these pioneering individuals laid down the foundation for future generations of Black Republicans.

Booker T. Washington and the Conservative Tradition:

In the early 20th century, Booker T. Washington became an iconic figure known for advocating education and economic self-sufficiency. A staunch Republican himself, Washington stressed practical skills as ways to foster racial progress; his philosophy resonated strongly among Black Republicans who believed individual self-improvement and entrepreneurial endeavor were keys to social advancement.

Civil Rights and the Republican Party:

The mid-20th century marked an inflection point in the relationship between Republican politics and civil rights activism. Although Democrats became synonymous with the advancement of rights, several influential Black Republican members played vital roles in fighting for equal opportunities within their Party; A. Philip Randolph, Bayard Rustin, and Jackie Robinson all challenged status quo Republicans while advocating reform within them to push towards social equality within Republican ranks and bring attention to its significance for justice among ethnic communities.

Black Republicans as Agents of Change:

Over the last several decades, black Republicans have increasingly distinguished themselves within their party as agents of change. From politicians like Condoleezza Rice, Colin Powell, and Tim Scott to grassroots activists and community leaders they have championed policies promoting economic opportunity, criminal justice reform, educational choice, and empowerment of marginalized communities - contributing significantly to party platforms while inspiring important discussions regarding race identity and conservative principles.

Contemporary Challenges and Opportunities for Black Republicans:

Black Republican history provides us with insight into their contemporary challenges and opportunities. Like any political organization, the Republican Party does face issues related to race inclusivity and representation - Black Republicans continue working within it to address such challenges, striving for greater diversity, understanding, and unity, amplifying voices while changing narratives; innovating narratives while crossing ideological divides while making sure their ancestral influences continue having impactful stories to tell.

Conclusion:

The history of Black Republicans in America is an inspiring testament to their resilience, courage, and transformative power as individuals who have helped shape the political dialogue and drive social progress forward since the Reconstruction era. From Reconstruction until today's present-day world of the internet and mobile phones, these pioneering individuals have contributed their voices against injustice by advocating for individual liberties such as individual self-determination and racial progress principles based on individual liberty, self-determination, racial progress - thus serving as inspirations to future generations who look to this rich legacy to shape political identity and action today.

CHAPTER 3: Political Awakening: Finding a Home in the Republican Party

Establishing our political identities and awakening to politics are transformative experiences for Black Republicans who wish to join the Republican Party, often from within its ranks. Here, we embark on an investigative journey of self-discovery and exploration as we examine factors contributing to Black individuals deciding to align themselves with this party; from personal experiences and ideological considerations affecting this decision as well as motivations behind political awakening itself.

Discovering Conservative Values:

Many Black Republicans' political awakening begins with an appreciation or new understanding of conservative principles such as limited government intervention, individual liberty, and personal responsibility. Individuals start exploring these principles more and find

an alignment with those espoused by the Republican Party -
while free markets, entrepreneurship, and self-
determination often play key roles. They realize how
conservative principles empower individuals and
communities towards self-sufficiency and upward mobility.

Personal Experiences Can Shape Political Awakening:

One's life experiences and observations can have an
enormous effect on their political awakening. Many Black
Republicans have encountered situations that challenge
conventional narratives and offer different viewpoints -
whether this means experiencing excessive bureaucracy,
seeing unintended effects from well-intentioned policies, or
witnessing individual efforts and determination yield
positive results - that prompt a realization that conservative
principles provide solutions for social and economic
challenges while giving individuals control of their
destinies. These encounters usually inspire realizations
about conservative principles' power as solutions versus

liberal ones - which often spark the realization that conservative principles offer solutions versus these experiences that help individuals take charge of their destinies.

Examining Historical Context:

Delving into history has long played an essential part in Black Republicans' political awakenings. Through studying its lessons from history, individuals gain a better grasp of society as it is today and its effects. Learning about historical figures like Frederick Douglass, Booker T. Washington and others who advocated for individual independence gives rise to feelings of inspiration; at the same time recognizing Republican Party history's commitments towards civil rights and equality strengthens these bonds between personal values and political ideology, thus giving rise to their identity as Black Republicans today.

Community and Mentorship:

Engaging with fellow conservatives, as well as consulting respected members within the Black Republican community can provide powerful catalysts in the political awakening process. Discussing ideas with these individuals provides invaluable insights. Mentorship relationships provide support, encouragement, and direction on a political journey. Sharing ideas and personal narratives within our communities provides individuals with a safe space to discover their political identities, identify a political home, and foster growth as we navigate the complexities of political engagement. These relationships serve as the cornerstone for success - helping each of us navigate its complexity together.

Overcoming Stereotypes and Misconceptions:

Black Republicans face one of the greatest challenges associated with their political identity - that of navigating and dispelling stereotypes and misconceptions associated with being Republicans. Doing this requires resilience, patience, and an open mindset as part of an awakening journey which includes challenging preconceived notions while engaging in constructive dialogue with people holding different political beliefs than their own. By sharing personal stories about why conservative values were chosen or showing diversity within the Party they can help dispel stereotypes while building understanding; through empathy-fueled dialogue, bridges may be built, and myths can be dismantled.

Acceptance Within the Republican Party:

The Republican Party, like any political organization, is dynamic and diverse in nature. Black Republicans play an essential role in advocating for increased diversity and inclusion within our party by participating actively in party activities, seeking leadership positions within our ranks, and supporting diverse candidates - contributing towards creating a more representative and welcoming Republican environment for everyone involved and engaged. Our involvement and engagement allow us to remain at the core of Republicanism for future generations of voters to come. By celebrating diversity within our party and emphasizing its relevance for all Americans, we foster an inclusive atmosphere where every voice can be heard and recognized as equal.

Conclusion:

For Black Republicans, political awakening can be an intensely personal and transformative journey. Through self-reflection, exploration of conservative values, personal experiences, historical context, community engagement, and challenging stereotypes we find an identity within the Republican Party that recognizes our unique perspectives and experiences - enriching it while creating a more inclusive political landscape. Together as members, we continue our political awakening while shaping it through

advocating diversity advocacy efforts, fostering

understanding initiatives, and working toward shared goals

- we stand united as Americans facing political awakening

together towards creating a brighter future for all

Americans.

Chapter 4: Facing the Dual Narrative: Challenges of Identity as a Black Republican

Being a Black Republican in America presents its

own set of unique challenges. Navigating this complex

intersection between racial identity and political ideology

presents its own set of difficulties that we will explore

further here. Our journey involves self-reflection and

discovery as we probe into this dual narrative experienced

by Black Republicans today and identify the multiple layers

of challenges, conflicts, and opportunities they encounter

on this path toward resilience, authenticity, and advocacy.

As Black Republicans, we often face an unfair burden of society's expectations of us. Black identity has often been associated with progressivism and loyalty to Democratic political candidates - an association we take great pains not to perpetuate. Emerging outside this narrative may bring with it suspicion, judgment, and even exclusion; thus requiring us to navigate these expectations while remaining true to our principles and ideals. Defying societal norms and adopting political ideologies that reflect our values takes courage and conviction, but doing so contributes to an ever-evolving political thought space and broadens what it means to be Black in America.

Political Stereotypes and Misperceptions:

Black Republicans often face political stereotypes and misconceptions which compromise our beliefs, degrading their authenticity and leading to inauthentic politics. Assumptions that all Black individuals must support progressive ideologies can obscure our individual experiences and perspectives, leading us to question racial stereotypes suggesting we betray our identity by adhering to more conservative principles. We must disprove them. Through respectful dialogue, we can inform others about the diversity of ideas and experiences within Black Republican society. By sharing stories and perspectives we break down barriers, foster understanding, and redefine what it means to be a Black Republican.

Reconciling Personal Experiences with Broader Narratives:

Black Republicans strive to strike a delicate balance in reconciling our individual experiences with wider narratives related to race and politics. Individual journeys, informed by our unique backgrounds, may deviate from or challenge commonly accepted narratives. While acknowledging systemic inequities and historical injustices, we also acknowledge personal agency, self-determination, and potential upward mobility as powerful assets. Es is necessary to present an inclusive perspective that acknowledges our experiences while advocating for policies and principles which empower individuals to overcome any hurdles they might be experiencing. By doing this, we foster a better understanding of Black life in America as an integrated whole.

Maintaining our Authenticity:

Being true to ourselves as Black Republicans requires being true to ourselves politically in terms of beliefs and actions, resisting pressure to conform, or adopting one-dimensional viewpoints. Engaging our diverse backgrounds, experiences, and ideologies strengthens our community while adding depth to political dialogue. Staying true to ourselves and sharing authentic narratives helps create a multifaceted picture of Black Republicans, emphasizing our diverse identities while showing that conservatism can coexist with social progressivism. Staying authentic allows us to present an inclusive narrative that represents all voices present within

Black Republicanism.

Navigating the Challenges of Identity as a Black

Republican also presents opportunities to build bridges and

find common ground with others. We pride ourselves on

engaging in constructive dialogue across political

spectrums to foster understanding and challenge

assumptions, seeking common values and goals as means

of unifying people across differences and building bridges

towards unity. Empathy, active listening, and respectful

communication are essential in creating coalitions and

effecting positive changes within communities and the

political arena. By engaging in meaningful discussions on

topics we agree upon and finding areas for agreement

across political divides, we can find lasting solutions that

benefit all Americans.

Advocacy and Representation:

As Black Republicans, we have the responsibility of advocating for policies that strengthen communities and advance equality. Representation matters; our voices play an integral part in crafting policy agendas to meet all Americans' needs and aspirations. Through political activism, community outreach activities, and advocacy for policies such as economic opportunity, educational equity, and criminal justice reform we can drive significant change that challenges the idea that conservatism cannot co-exist with social progress - thus upholding conservatism's core ideals while remaining inclusive to diverse communities' interests and needs. Our advocacy helps shape and represents us throughout its long history - helping ensure its relevance over time.

Conclusion:

Black Republicans face unique and complex identity hurdles when navigating identity, yet these challenges are surmountable. By acknowledging and responding to both narratives simultaneously, resilience, authenticity, and advocacy can flourish. By challenging societal expectations and dispelling stereotypes while reconciling personal experiences with larger narratives we must stay true to ourselves while challenging societal expectations, dispelling political stereotypes, reconciling personal experience with narratives shared widely and remaining authentic to ourselves - we will ultimately create a more equitable and inclusive society - Black Republicans hold immense power that allows us to redefine political norms while shaping discourse - contributing directly towards creating an inclusive and equitable society which acknowledges both identities while giving voice to all voices heard within its fold.

Chapter 5: Navigating Partisanship: Building Bridges across Political Divides

Introduction:

Navigating partisanship is a vital aspect of being a Black Republican in America. It requires us to bridge political divides, foster understanding, and engage in constructive dialogue with individuals from different political backgrounds. In this chapter, we embark on a journey of collaboration and empathy, exploring the challenges and opportunities that arise when seeking common ground across partisan lines. By navigating partisanship with an open mind, a commitment to collaboration, and a friendly demeanor, we can foster unity and create positive change in our communities and the political landscape.

Understanding the Value of Empathy:

Empathy serves as a powerful tool in navigating partisanship. It involves stepping into the shoes of others and genuinely seeking to understand their perspectives, values, and concerns. When we approach political discussions with empathy, we cultivate a deeper appreciation for the diverse experiences and beliefs of individuals from different political ideologies. This understanding helps bridge the gap between political affiliations, enabling us to find areas of commonality and shared goals. By practicing empathy, we create a space for respectful dialogue, establish a foundation for building bridges, and foster collaboration across partisan divides.

Active Listening: Seeking to Understand:

Active listening is a cornerstone of effective communication and a valuable skill in navigating partisanship. It involves setting aside preconceived notions and truly engaging with the perspectives of others. When we actively listen, we demonstrate a genuine desire to understand the viewpoints of individuals from different political backgrounds. By actively listening, we validate the experiences and beliefs of others, even if they differ from our own. This approach allows us to identify common ground, find points of agreement, and foster productive conversations. Through active listening, we build trust, demonstrate respect, and create an environment that promotes understanding and cooperation.

Respectful Communication: Finding Common Language:

Respectful communication is crucial in bridging political divides. It involves expressing our ideas and opinions in a manner that is respectful, constructive, and inclusive. When engaging in political discussions, we should choose our words carefully, ensuring they convey our thoughts without resorting to personal attacks or divisive language. Respectful communication also means being open to different perspectives and being willing to challenge our own beliefs. By fostering an atmosphere of respect and inclusivity, we create an environment that encourages meaningful dialogue and collaboration. Through respectful communication, we can find a common language, bridge divides, and work towards shared goals.

Identifying Shared Values and Goals:

Navigating partisanship requires us to identify shared values and goals that transcend political affiliations. While we may differ on specific policy solutions, there are often broader objectives that we can all agree upon. As Black Republicans, we share a commitment to justice, equality, and opportunity. By focusing on these shared values, we can build bridges and work towards common objectives. This approach allows us to move beyond partisan labels and focus on the positive change we can achieve together. By finding common ground, we build trust, create momentum for collaboration, and foster unity.

Seeking Collaborative Solutions:

Navigating partisanship involves seeking collaborative solutions that address the needs and aspirations of all Americans. By engaging in bipartisan or cross-partisan initiatives, we demonstrate a commitment to effective governance and problem-solving. Collaborative solutions often require compromise, as we work towards finding common ground and meeting the diverse needs of our communities. However, these solutions yield the most sustainable and impactful outcomes. By bringing diverse perspectives to the table and working towards shared goals, we can transcend political divides and create positive change that benefits our communities and the nation as a whole. Seeking collaborative solutions is an opportunity for us to lead by example, fostering a culture of unity and cooperation.

Leading by Example:

As Black Republicans, we can lead by example in navigating partisanship.

By demonstrating a commitment to respectful dialogue, empathy, and collaborative problem-solving, we can inspire others to do the same. Our actions can serve as a model for constructive engagement and bridge-building, fostering a

culture of unity, understanding, and cooperation. By

leading by example, we contribute to a more inclusive and

productive political landscape, where differences are

respected, diverse perspectives are valued, and

collaboration is prioritized for the greater good.

Conclusion:

Navigating partisanship as Black Republicans is

both a challenge and an opportunity. By approaching

political divides with empathy, active listening, and

respectful communication, we can build bridges and find

common ground. By focusing on shared values and goals,

seeking collaborative solutions, and leading by example,

we create positive change and foster unity. Our ability to

navigate partisanship is essential in shaping the future of

our communities and the nation, where political differences

are transcended in favor of collective progress. Through

friendly and constructive dialogue, we can bridge the gaps

that divide us and work towards a more inclusive and
harmonious society.

Chapter 6: Advocacy and Activism: Making a Difference within the Republican Party

Intro:

Advocacy and activism are vital tools for driving meaningful change within the Republican Party, providing Black Republicans an incredible opportunity to make lasting impacts by participating in advocacy initiatives aligned with our values and meeting community needs. In this chapter, we delve into advocacy's significance while outlining effective strategies as well as any challenges or hurdles we might come across along our journey -

harnessing collective voices together we can shape this

party for greater inclusion, equality, and prosperity in

society as a whole.

Understanding Advocacy:

Advocacy allows us to use our voices, resources,

and influence for positive change within the Republican

Party. Advocacy provides us a tool for driving economic

opportunity, educational equity reforms, criminal justice

reform, and healthcare access initiatives affecting Black

communities directly addressing our unique barriers and

needs as Black Americans - amplifying concerns while

advocating solutions & creating positive impacts within it

all.

Identification of Key Issues:

To effectively advocate for change, we must

identify those key issues which align with our values and

have direct ramifications on our communities. To effectively do so requires doing thorough research, engaging in dialogue with fellow Black Republicans, staying updated about current events, and understanding any challenges our communities are experiencing; whether systemic racism, economic disparities, or educational inequities. By targeting our advocacy efforts on specific key issues such as these we can make targeted, impactful progress toward change.

Building Alliances and Collaborations:

Advocacy becomes far more effective when we form alliances and form coalitions with like-minded people, organizations, and communities. By uniting forces with other Black Republicans, community leaders, advocacy groups, grassroots organizations, or grassroots campaigns -- such as Black Republican organizations - and community activists for change we can increase our effectiveness significantly by amplifying impact through collective action utilizing shared resources, expertise, expertise shared between various stakeholder, as well as strengthening networks within our political party itself -- we can leverage all strengths. By coming together we can achieve far more than our efforts could ever achieve alone.

Utilizing Multiple Advocacy Strategies:

There's no one-size-fits-all approach to advocacy or activism; therefore, a variety of advocacy strategies must be employed to effectively reach our target audiences and drive change. Strategies such as grassroots organizing, engaging elected officials in policy debates, organizing outreach/education campaigns, participating in public demonstrations, social media advocacy strategies as well as using our tools can all contribute effectively towards our advocacy goals; each has unique benefits tailored towards meeting them individually with success allowing us to reach different audiences while creating awareness/mobilizing support/effect change on multiple fronts.

Engaging Elected Officials:

Engaging elected officials is an integral component of advocacy within the Republican Party. Through developing relationships with Republican representatives, senators, and policymakers we can influence policy priorities from within by attending town hall meetings, and campaign events, establishing personal connections with them and their staff as well as making firsthand contributions and data-backed arguments on our chosen issues that promote equality, justice, and opportunity for all.

Amplifying Our Voices through Media: Media can be an incredible platform for advocacy and activism. By harnessing social media platforms, writing op-eds for newspapers, or appearing on news programs ourselves we can amplify our voices to shape public narratives by sharing personal accounts of experiences or issues relevant to a cause we care deeply about. By telling our own personal tales through story sharing or media exposure we can amplify and shape public dialogue about issues important to us all - be they environmental, cultural or socially charged issues we can amplify and amplifying voices within public discourses which help amplify and shape public narratives while sharing personal accounts can amplify voices that shape public narratives with their personal experiences has an immense power when used strategically by sharing personal accounts or appearing on news programs which helps share personal accounts that highlight issues in public dialogues around issues which arisen at stake as well as sharing personal accounts can amplify voices that shape public narratives by sharing personal accounts/expel/experience/shared experiences/ sharing personal accounts can amp up amp/share personal/experience sharing from personal/sharing stories shared experiences/ experiences shared from personal stories shared from personal narratives shared can influence public narratives/share/ share experiences sharing personal accounts through sharing of personal accounts such as these shared by sharing individual/sharer stories by public figures/appearance on news programs/appearance/appearance thus ample/voice- by sharing personal accounts/appearance or shaping the public narrative by public media outlets through sharing personal accounts that allow sharing our story/sharing stories/ sharing experiences/sharing of life/share stories to provide publics/ sharing/share sharing shared stories by someone/ sharing's shared.

Policy proposals, media programs, and policy advice allow us to challenge stereotypes, bridge divides, and increase understanding. Media gives us access to a wider audience, engages dialogues with them, and inspires more to join our cause. When utilized effectively media can raise awareness, rally support from its participants, and mobilize communities toward change.

Overcoming Challenges:

Advocacy and activism do not come without their challenges, with resistance, criticism, and setbacks likely along the way. Anticipating and planning for potential hurdles to advocacy or activism is vital if we want to succeed - building resilience while keeping the focus on goals is also necessary, along with finding support networks within both the Republican Party and community networks - this ensures lasting change by remaining true to our values, approaching obstacles with positivity in mind, seeking common ground between perspectives whose perspectives might initially clash, helping us overcome barriers while further creating meaningful change together.

Conclusion:

Advocacy and activism can make an enormous difference within the Republican Party. By understanding the significance of our voices, identifying key issues, building alliances, employing diverse advocacy strategies, engaging elected officials, and using media platforms, we can use our voices to shape policy, foster inclusivity and create an equitable society. While challenges will always exist, our dedication to our values and collaborative advocacy efforts will bring about the change we seek. Let's continue being champions for progress within the Republican Party to have an immediate positive impactful on both communities and nations alike; together we can create a brighter, more prosperous future for everyone.

Chapter 7: Upholding Conservative Values: The Intersection of Race and Ideology

Welcome to Chapter 7, where we investigate the intersection between race and ideology within the context of upholding conservative values. As Black Republicans, we embark on an extraordinary journey as we struggle to navigate our racial identities while staying true to conservative principles. Here, we will delve deeper into conservative principles' significance, reconciling race with conservative ideals, as well as contributing to more inclusive and diverse conservative movements. Let's dive in together to discover how our heritage shapes political perspectives.

Acknowledging Conservative Principles:

Conservative principles form the backbone of our ideology. These encompass such ideas as limited government, individual freedom, free markets, and personal responsibility. These principles emphasize the value of self-reliance, entrepreneurship, and equal access to opportunities for all. As Black Republicans, we believe in the ability of individuals to pursue their ambitions and

make their own choices - creating an environment in which

freedom of individual action and economic prosperity

flourish simultaneously. Adopting conservative values does

not equate to dismissing the issues facing our communities;

rather, it provides us with the means for working toward

creating an environment that respects individual rights,

rewards hard work, and promotes upward mobility for all.

Reconciling Race and Ideology: Exploring how best

to reconcile our racial identity and conservative ideology

can be a complex, emotional journey. Black Republicans

sometimes believe their conservative ideals don't align well

with struggles faced by our community and vice versa - this

notion often creates tension within us and can prevent

growth as Black Republicans. However, we recognize the

unique strengths offered by conservatism for addressing

social and economic challenges; its foundation rests upon

individual empowerment and self-determination leading to

long-term economic prosperity. At the same time, we recognize and acknowledge how historical events and systemic influences have affected Black Americans - by doing this we can advocate for policies within a conservative framework that promotes equality, justice, and opportunity for everyone.

Approaching Racial Inequities:

Conservative values provide us with the foundation needed for effectively addressing racial disparities and encouraging upward mobility within our communities. We support policies that promote economic development, entrepreneurial spirit, and educational choice - policies that conservative values promote as essential ingredients to social progress. These initiatives equip individuals to overcome barriers and reach success on their terms. By advocating policies to support small businesses, reduce regulatory burdens, and expand access to capital we can open economic doors while closing wealth gaps.

Furthermore, we understand the vital significance of criminal justice reform, educational equity, and revitalization to address systemic challenges disproportionately affecting Black Americans. Upholding conservative values does not equate to turning away from these problems - rather it requires finding creative solutions which reflect our principles.

As Black Republicans, we play an essential part in fostering diversity within the conservative movement. Our experiences, insights, and voices add depth and richness to dialogue about policy development that meets diverse American needs and aspirations. Through actively engaging in discussions about conservative values that transcend race as well as sharing perspectives that challenge preconceived notions about us all Americans - our presence serves as a powerful reminder that inclusivity is integral for strong and effective movements like ours.

Create Paths of Engagement:

To uphold conservative values and foster racial understanding, we must open pathways of dialogue. Actively joining local Republican organizations, attending party events, joining think tanks, or serving as mentors is one way of participating in shaping conservative agendas or policies - this also serves as a great opportunity to reach out and connect with young Black individuals by sharing our experiences and encouraging their involvement in conservatism as mentors - ultimately building bridges of understanding, empathy, and mutual respect to foster an even stronger conservative movement that truly represents everyone involved - uniting us as we advance and further unifying conservative movement that truly represents all its participants.

Diversity defines our nation:

Attaining conservative values while navigating the complex realms of race and ideology can be both challenging and exciting. We must embrace its principles while at the same time acknowledging our individual experiences of racial identity. By reconciling these aspects, we can foster an inclusive and vibrant conservative movement that addresses all Americans' needs and aspirations. Let us continue this path together by appreciating our history, upholding conservative values, and striving towards creating an equitable society that values individual liberty while offering equal opportunities and prioritizing citizen well-being. Together we can have a positive influence and help shape a brighter future for both communities and our nation.

Chapter 8: Campaigning and Elections: Experiences on the Campaign Trail

Welcome to Chapter 8, where we enter the electrifying world of campaigning and elections. As Black Republicans, campaign trails provide exciting experiences rife with excitement, challenges, and meaningful connections between us and our communities. In this chapter we will dive deep into running for office: building strong teams; engaging voters and understanding the political landscape; fundraising successfully for causes we care about; overthrowing challenges through fundraising strategies and celebrating victories. So, fasten your seatbelts for an insightful journey into political campaigns' ups and downs.

At its heart lies a fundamental desire to serve, an urge that drives many of us towards running for office as public servants and our commitment to represent those whose values we represent - either locally, state-wide, or nationally - by advocating on their behalf and creating lasting change within society. Our campaigns serve as platforms through which to bring about these changes with impactful campaigns across these levels of government.

Building a Strong Team:

Behind every successful campaign lies an exceptional and diverse team, brought together around one shared vision. Black Republicans bring special perspectives, talents, and experiences that enhance its strategies and messaging. Campaign managers to communications specialists to volunteers play integral roles in our campaign's success while nurturing an inclusive and collaborative atmosphere that creates an environment in which each member's skillsets are appreciated, ideas welcomed, and diverse viewpoints heard.

Engaging Voters:

Campaigns are all about developing relationships between voters, understanding their concerns, and building genuine bonds between each candidate and them. Black Republicans bring with us unique experiences and perspectives which resonate within communities throughout our state; therefore we engage in community forums, town hall meetings, and door-to-door canvassing to listen attentively to constituent needs through community forums, town hall meetings, and door-to-door canvassing events to determine these needs firsthand and establish trust while strengthening ties by actively engaging our voters; through doing this we demonstrate our dedication in representing their interests.

Navigating the Political Landscape:

Navigating the political landscape can be both exhilarating and daunting for Black Republicans, who may encounter unique hurdles and misconceptions as we campaign. We must remain true to our core beliefs that our ideas can create positive change through inclusive issue-focused campaigns which break down barriers, challenge stereotypes, demonstrate diversity within our Republican Party strengthens democracy - we navigate with grace resilience determination to make lasting impacts within society.

Fundraising and Resource Mobilization:

Running an effective campaign requires financial resources. Fundraising and resource mobilization are essential parts of campaign strategy; as Black Republicans we have the unique opportunity of reaching out across various networks and engaging individuals who share our vision, providing our message effectively while connecting donors directly. Through traditional and creative fundraising methods alike we create a solid financial base on which to run campaigns that reach wider audiences.

Campaigns don't come without their challenges; from physical exertion and emotional strains to encountering additional bias, stereotypes, or partisan political obstacles on our journeys as Black Republicans - yet these obstacles do not define us; instead, we remain focused on our goals, maintain positive thoughts, rely on team support from colleagues and rely on community backing as a strong base - by rising above adversity we become stronger individuals determined to make change happen.

At the Core of Successful Campaigns:

Grassroots organizing lies at the core of effective campaigns. Individuals coming together, mobilizing volunteers, and planning community events that create momentum toward victory is what fuels grassroots organizing's power to generate results. As Black Republicans, we leverage the strength of community connections, cultural ties, and shared values to engage voters on an individual basis at grassroots levels. By engaging voters through genuine conversations and cultivating relationships and harnessing technology tools such as social media or technology platforms - Black Republicans extend their reach and increase support.

Celebrating Victories:

Every campaign has defining moments and victories worth celebrating, especially as Black Republicans. Our victories hold special meaning both within our communities and for the conservative movement as a whole, signifying progress by breaking barriers and challenging preconceived notions; by sharing stories of triumph, we also help inspire future generations of Black Republicans to step forward, follow their passion, and leave their mark on political history.

Conclusion:

Election campaigns present us with the unique chance to leave an impactful mark in our communities. Black Republicans provide vibrant and diverse voices on the campaign trail, further enriching political dialogue while inviting others to participate in democracy. By creating strong teams, engaging voters, navigating challenges successfully, and celebrating victories we contribute to creating an inclusive and representative political system. While victory may prove challenging at times, its journey can also bring joy, connection, and empowerment along the way. So let us raise our voices, run impactful campaigns, and strive towards creating an America where our communities, values, and voices are represented and heard. Together we can change the course of our nation and secure a brighter future for all.

Chapter 9: Building Coalitions: Collaborating with Diverse Communities

Welcome to Chapter 9, as we journey together towards building coalitions and collaboration among diverse communities as Black Republicans. In this chapter, we delve deeper into the strategies, benefits, and challenges associated with working alongside individuals from various walks of life to form more inclusive movements that reflect all aspects of American culture and history. By acknowledging diversity's strength while cultivating relationships through active listening techniques and amplifying underrepresented voices into political campaigns as Black Republicans we can forge stronger coalitions that reflect this nation as a whole - so let us discover together its power through building coalitions among diverse communities in friendship and understanding.

Recognizing Diversity's Strength:

Diversity isn't simply a buzzword - Black Republicans recognize and deeply value its strength as an asset to our movement. By welcoming diverse perspectives, experiences, and backgrounds we increase understanding while broadening impact - each individual and community brings with them unique talents, ideas, insights, and expertise that makes our movement stronger overall. By actively seeking collaboration across diverse communities, we tap into an invaluable source of collective intelligence while creating a stronger conservative movement overall.

Finding Common Ground:

Building coalitions requires finding areas of agreement among people outside our traditional networks. We should seek issues that resonate across communities while exploring areas of mutual interest; by emphasizing our shared aspirations for economic prosperity, individual liberty, strong families, and safer neighborhoods we can bridge ideological divisions and find ways to collaborate on finding positive change through coalition building based on shared goals.

Fostering Relationships and Trust:

Effective collaboration relies upon strong interpersonal bonds between participants. At Black Republicans, we recognize the significance of cultivating meaningful connections among community members from diverse backgrounds by participating in events, engaging with organizations, and creating an open forum of conversation. By investing both time and energy into creating these meaningful bonds between us all, trust will develop over time not overnight.

Engaging in Active Listening:

Listening is an invaluable skill when building coalitions. Active listening involves not simply hearing what others say but understanding their perspectives, experiences, and concerns as well. Engaging in active listening shows our commitment to inclusivity and understanding while creating an environment in which individuals feel heard, validated, and respected. Engaging in active listening also allows us to understand the unique challenges facing different communities so we can tailor our approaches accordingly and develop policies that meet everyone's diverse needs in society.

Respect Cultural Sensitivities:

Cultural sensitivity is at the core of effective coalition-building. By honoring the cultural practices, beliefs, and values of communities we engage with we create an environment in which individuals feel welcomed and appreciated as members. Understanding different cultural perspectives and customs sensitivities ensures collaborative processes run more smoothly while strengthening an overall sense of belonging within coalitions.

Reducing Challenges and Building Trust:

Forming coalitions across diverse communities can present unique obstacles. Historical tensions, misconceptions, or political differences may initially present barriers. At Black Republicans, we approach such difficulties with patience, empathy, and a genuine desire to understand. By engaging in open and honest dialogues that directly address concerns directly as well as seeking common ground solutions wherever possible; transparency integrity consistent engagement are keys to meeting challenges head-on while forging bonds within our coalitions.

Amplifying Underrepresented Voices:

Black Republicans offer an invaluable opportunity for amplifying underrepresented communities within the conservative movement by actively promoting diverse leaders, encouraging participation, and celebrating diversity within our ranks. We actively work on increasing participation. Assuring all communities have an equal say ensures our movement truly represents its diversity, which ultimately strengthens coalitions and movements alike. By amplifying underrepresented voices, we foster inclusivity by opening space for diverse viewpoints while strengthening coalitions as a whole. By amplifying underrepresented voices, we foster inclusivity by amplifying underrepresented voices and fostering inclusiveness by increasing representation across our coalition while guaranteeing all voices have equal representation at our table thereby strengthening coalitions while representing every aspect of diversity that makes up America today.

Conclusion:

Black Republicans recognize that building coalitions and working collaboratively with diverse communities is both their obligation and an exciting opportunity. By welcoming diversity, embracing commonalities among different identities, cultivating relationships, engaging in active listening sessions, respecting cultural sensitivities, and amplifying underrepresented voices we create a more inclusive movement and can collectively achieve greater impact by meeting society's varied needs and creating an equitable future for us all to share in. So let us continue building friendships across divides to foster understanding between cultures while working collaboratively underpinned by mutual trust in pursuit of our shared future. Let us continue building alliances among diverse communities while engaging actively within ourselves by respect for one another so we may truly achieve a greater impact at creating more equitable societies than before and build our nation together. Let us collaborate in a spirit of friendship, understanding, respect, and togetherness for the betterment of us all and ensure success.

Chapter 10: Promoting Policy Change: Legislative Impact and Policy Initiatives

Welcome to Chapter 10, where we embark on our journey of policy change as Black Republicans. In this chapter, we investigate the legislative impact and the value of policy initiatives to create lasting change within the communities we serve. By actively engaging with policy-making processes, advocating conservative principles, and championing innovative solutions - such as making our voices heard about conservative principles- we can leave lasting impacts upon the lives we touch. So, let's dive deeper into strategies, challenges, and opportunities involved with advocating policy reform via legislative action.

Understanding Policy's Transformative Force:

The policy is more than a list of rules; it has the power to transform our society for good. Black Republicans recognize this and understand its profound effects on individuals, families, and communities - from stimulating economic growth and safeguarding individual liberties to confronting pressing social issues with thoughtful solutions that reflect conservative principles while elevating those we represent. By actively participating in policy development processes, we hold great power to shape its trajectory for ourselves and all nations around us.

Research and Analysis:

Promoting policy change demands extensive research and analysis. To build successful arguments for change, researchers need the evidence needed to make their case. Conducting rigorous studies, studying best practices, and analyzing data allow us to equip ourselves with the knowledge necessary for crafting compelling arguments for policy reform backed up with compelling arguments for change backed up with compelling facts that strengthen the credibility and effectiveness of advocacy campaigns supporting them.

Building coalitions is a crucial tactic for advancing policy reform. When working together with like-minded individuals, organizations, and interest groups we amp up our collective voice and expand our influence. Coalition building brings different people under a shared policy agenda with different perspectives, expertise, and resources available. By finding common ground we strengthen advocacy efforts bringing positive reform that affects all. By joining forces together as one powerful force we can drive reform that benefits us all - regardless of party lines.

Engaging With Legislators:

Direct engagement with legislators is central to policy reform efforts, opening opportunities for meaningful dialogue, influence, and impactful results. At town hall meetings and public hearings, we attend or schedule meetings with members of elected officials as we share personal stories to make compelling cases for policy reforms while forging meaningful relationships that foster trust with elected officials allowing us to effectively advocate for policies aligning with conservative principles. As Black Republicans, we possess an unparalleled opportunity and perspective when it comes to developing innovative policy initiatives to meet the needs of our communities. By drawing upon our diversity in terms of backgrounds and experiences, we can develop creative yet pragmatic solutions. We must engage in robust policy discussions while consulting subject matter experts as part of this development process; only then can we truly present well-crafted policy initiatives which reflect both conservative principles and realities in the communities we represent.

Messaging and Advocacy:

Effective messaging and advocacy are at the core of policy change efforts. To effectively promote policy reform, our policy proposals must resonate with diverse audiences while conveying their benefits - this means adapting messages that speak the language of those whom we're persuading while matching values with aspirations of target constituents - by tailoring messages directly for specific constituencies we can build support across party lines as well as engaging those outside our political ideology who may initially feel alienated by political rhetoric alone - effective messaging can create understanding while building coalitions while mobilizing support behind policies which can make meaningful change happen.

Navigating Challenges:

Promoting policy change does not come without its share of obstacles and opposition from some sources. As resilient Black Republicans, we understand that political infighting, bureaucratic hurdles, and setbacks may thwart our progress. Yet as determined and strategic thinkers we approach such obstacles with determination. By forging coalitions with allies who share common ground as well as by maintaining a long-term perspective and staying informed to adapt strategies, when necessary, we are better able to overcome any potential setbacks while continuing to advance policy priorities.

Conclusion:

Black Republicans recognize the significance of creating legislative impact through advocacy for policy change and advancement as one of their core missions. Through messaging, coalition-building, engagement with legislators, creating innovative policy initiatives, and effective messaging we have the power to effect meaningful changes that benefit those we represent and enhance their lives. Let us approach this task together with an openness toward collaboration and dialogue so that together we can shape a future aligned with conservative principles, uplift communities, and provide equal access to opportunities for all.

Chapter 11: Media and Representation: Black Republicans in the Public Eye

Welcome to Chapter 11, where we delve deep into the world of media and representation for Black Republicans. In this chapter, we examine the challenges, opportunities, and strategies associated with successfully navigating the media landscape as we attempt to promote conservative values while amplifying our voices as public figures. As public figures, representation matters: by actively engaging the media and championing diverse voices within our party we can challenge stereotypes while building understanding - inspiring others to join our cause. So come with us on this exciting adventure of media and representation with an optimistic spirit ready to create lasting change. Let's embark together and make lasting impacts together.

Media Power:

Media can have tremendous sway over public opinion and political dialogue, so as Black Republicans, we must recognize and harness its immense force to advance our cause. Through various media platforms like television, radio, print media, and digital media platforms we have an invaluable opportunity to express ourselves freely: sharing experiences that define who we are; discussing policy positions at length with reporters from television stations to newspapers to digital outlets like Snapchat - by actively engaging the media our voices will be heard more fully represented within public conversations and policy debates.

Representation Matters:

Being represented matters and as Black Republicans, we play an essential part in shattering stereotypes and dispelling false impressions about our party and communities. By actively seeking opportunities to represent ourselves and our constituents in media outlets we can challenge one-dimensional depictions by providing more nuanced depictions which reflect both diversity and strength of ideas within our ranks.

Building Media Relationships:

Cultivating solid relationships with media professionals is paramount to effectively communicating our message and shaping public opinion. By forging close ties with journalists, editors, and producers we establish trust, foster mutual understanding, and increase the odds of fair and accurate representation. By engaging in open and respectful dialogue and providing reliable information we ensure our voices become part of broader media conversations.

Crafting an Effective Message:

Crafting an impactful message is central to successfully engaging with media outlets and reaching a broad array of audiences. As Black Republicans, we offer unique perspectives which bridge gaps while connecting with individuals from diverse backgrounds. Clarifying our policy positions effectively by employing language that is inclusive, relatable, and solution-focused is of vital importance. By emphasizing shared values such as personal responsibility, economic empowerment, and individual liberty we can find common ground while making an influential case for conservative principles. Sharing real-life stories that show the positive results of policies created through conservatism helps humanize our message further and build deeper bonds between ourselves and the public.

Utilizing social media and Digital Platforms:

Today's digital age provides us with powerful tools for amplifying our voices and reaching a larger audience through platforms like Twitter, Facebook, Instagram, and YouTube. Through platforms such as these, we are directly accessible to supporters as well as critics; offering access for sharing experiences, advocating policy initiatives, or engaging in meaningful discussions - such as through platforms such as these. It is key that our presence be consistent yet authentic while adhering to ethical guidelines while engaging in respectful discourse on these platforms to increase our influence beyond traditional media outlets.

By effectively employing these social media tools we can expand our reach by cultivating loyal followings beyond traditional media outlets while shaping public opinion beyond traditional media outlets.

Navigating Challenges:

Engaging with media as Black Republicans can present significant difficulties, from biased coverage and misinterpretation to hostile interviews. But we must face these difficulties with resilience, grace, and commitment to our principles - in particular by clarifying misconceptions with facts or correcting inaccuracies - thus furthering the education of the public at large while adhering to our core values and priorities. Together we can effectively navigate these difficulties and foster understanding even under duress.

Conclusion:

Media and representation play an instrumental role in shaping public opinion and shaping the narrative surrounding our party and conservative values. Black Republicans can use media engagement and representation strategically, actively challenging stereotypes, ensuring our voices and perspectives are heard by actively engaging with media, challenging stereotypes, building strong media relationships, crafting effective messages on social media platforms such as Twitter, or using resilient resilience strategies when facing obstacles, to effectively spread our message, inspire others, promote inclusive political debate. Let us seize this moment to be agents of change within the media landscape and allow our voices to be heard loud and clear.

Chapter 12: Inspiring the Next Generation: Mentoring and Youth Engagement

Welcome to Chapter 12, where we embark on an exciting adventure of inspiring the next generation as Black

Republicans. As leaders within our party, we possess an immense opportunity to make an enduring positive difference in young lives through mentorship. In this chapter, we'll delve deeper into its power as well as strategies for engaging youth, and the transformative potential we hold over their future - creating an environment conducive to growth, empowerment, and inclusivity while inspiring future Black Republican generations.

Mentorship Can Shape Young Lives and Perspectives: Mentorship can play a powerful role in shaping young lives and perspectives. Black Republicans can serve as mentors by offering guidance, wisdom, and support as young individuals navigate life and politics with our conservative values and understandings of success and failure - this way encouraging and motivating our younger members to embrace conservative principles while emphasizing active participation within democracy itself.

Engaging With Youth:

Fostering youth engagement in conservative values and politics requires engaging directly with young people at local community events, schools, universities, and youth organizations. Panel discussions, workshops, and educational programs create spaces where young voices are heard and respected - as do actively listening to concerns expressed by our young people as we address their questions about how conservative principles align with their hopes and ambitions and can impact lives positively in communities worldwide.

Leading by Example:

One of the most impactful ways of inspiring future leaders is by setting an example through our actions and accomplishments as Black Republicans. Through active political participation, community service efforts, and championing causes aligned with conservative ideals we

become living examples of conservative ideals'
transformative power; our integrity, compassion, and
dedication inspire young individuals to embrace
conservative ideals themselves and motivate them into
becoming future leaders themselves.

Establish Mentorship Programs:

To maximize our impact, it's vitally important that
our party establish tailored mentorship programs tailored
specifically for young individuals within our party.
Through regular meetings and mentorship activities with
young mentees as mentees advance, experienced Black
Republicans connect and guide young mentees while
forging meaningful bonds which provide invaluable
support and guidance - not to mention creating an
atmosphere of belonging that inspires future Republicans to
participate more fully in our party's future. Mentorship
programs not only foster personal development, but they

create a sense of belonging that encourages active involvement in our party's future.

Encourage Political Participation:

Fostering Political Participation among Young Individuals is vitally important to our party and democracy, both locally and at an international level. By actively encouraging student government memberships, local political positions, internship opportunities, and campaign activities; providing guidance and mentorship as needed, and hands-on experience will enable young leaders from diverse backgrounds to develop the necessary knowledge, confidence, and skill set to lead effectively - we foster an atmosphere that embraces these unique perspectives from young members within the party and ensure they all feel welcome, appreciated and welcome within our party culture.

Empowering Young Republicans:

We should try to recognize, value, and uphold the voices of young Republicans to give them an outlet to express their thoughts, ideas, and concerns. By providing opportunities for them to do this at events geared toward youth such as town hall meetings or panel discussions we create an atmosphere in which their voices can be amplified and valued; actively soliciting input and including it in party initiatives not only increases participation but fosters ownership and empowerment of members alike - by doing this we create an organization which is dynamic yet inclusive - reflective of all communities we aim to serve.

Conclusion:

Sparked to create the next generation of Black Leaders Mentorship and youth engagement represent an admirable effort that holds immense promise for Republicans as an organization and our country. By offering mentorship services, engaging youth, leading by example, creating mentorship programs, encouraging political participation, empowering voices of youth participants in Republican events and programs, and creating mentorship programs aimed at youth, we create an atmosphere of growth, empowerment, and inclusivity in which Republican ideals may flourish for generations yet unborn - torchbearers that will take forward our conservative values into the future of both parties and our country alike. Together let us shoulder our responsibility of inspiring and leading next-generation Republican youth members since their values will shape both parties and the country.

Chapter 13: Overcoming Adversity: Resilience in the Face of Opposition

Welcome to Chapter 13, where we explore overcoming adversity as Black Republicans. At various points in our journeys, we encounter various forms of opposition which test our resilience and determination, yet these moments present us with the chance to show our strength, resilience, and unwavering commitment to values and ideals. Here, we will cover various types of resistance encountered along our path; strategies for building resilience; staying true to convictions even during difficult moments - everything needed for successful Black Republicanism.

As Black Republicans, we may face opposition from many sources: political rivals, social stereotypes, and members of our communities. To effectively navigate through such opposition we must recognize its source: acknowledging any ideological differences or misinformation at play as we approach any given situation with patience, empathy, and willingness for dialogue - understanding each opposer can create deeper insight and lead to productive dialogues between parties in opposition and us.

Develop Resilience:

Resilience is a valuable trait that enables us to overcome hardship and maintain our sense of purpose in challenging environments. Fostering resilience involves cultivating mental fortitude, emotional resilience, and the capacity for adapting quickly to changing situations. Cultivating it involves self-reflection and caregiving strategies designed specifically for challenging circumstances - developing these is essential when facing tough times alone; cultivating it also includes seeking guidance and support from friends, family members, or mentors that offer guidance and encouragement along the way. In doing so we can face down challenges head-on and emerge stronger than before than ever.

Staying True to Our Convictions:

In the face of opposition, we must adhere to our convictions and core values. While criticism or negative rhetoric might tempt us away from sticking by what we believe in, remaining firm in our beliefs allows us to inspire others and bring about meaningful change. By communicating clearly about these conservative principles-based values with conviction and authenticity we not only overcome adversity but challenge misconceptions or stereotypes which contributes to greater understanding and acceptance between communities.

Building Support Networks:

Network building can play an essential part in helping us face and overcome adversity. Surrounding ourselves with like-minded individuals who share our values and can empathize with our experiences can offer encouragement, guidance, and emotional support during difficult times. By cultivating relationships with fellow Black Republicans, allies, mentors, or any others who might help, we foster resilience while strengthening resilience at an individual and communal level - which allows us to confidently face adversity head-on. Sharing our stories and experiences as well as strategies against it can inspire and empower others going through similar circumstances.

Turn Adversity Into Opportunity:

Adversity can be an invaluable catalyst for positive growth and transformation. By reframing challenges as opportunities, we can harness their force for innovation, creativity, resilience, and transformation. Adversity often forces us out of our comfort zones, forcing us to find alternative paths toward success while unlocking the untapped potential within ourselves - when seen through this lens adversity becomes an opportunity. Embracing obstacles as tools of personal and professional growth we can turn obstacles into steppingstones on our journey toward greater success and fulfillment.

Promote Unity and Understanding:

At times of hardship, unity and understanding between our party and community members are of critical importance. Building bridges of communication and empathy to bridge any divides that might otherwise separate us and foster a sense of shared purpose; while actively searching for common ground with those holding different viewpoints can foster productive dialogue that brings about fruitful dialogue and collaborative pursuit of goals which bring people together towards breaking down barriers, challenging stereotypes, and creating more welcoming societies - we have to ensure everyone feels welcome and understood in society at large.

Conclusions:

Overcoming adversity as Black Republicans require resilience, determination, and an unyielding dedication to our values. By understanding and acknowledging the opposition's nature and building resilience through staying true to convictions and supportive networks while making use of challenges as opportunities, turning adversity into opportunity while encouraging unity and understanding we can navigate challenges more successfully and emerge stronger than before. Let us embrace resilience's powerful effects as we travel further along our journey and ensure a brighter future for ourselves and future generations.

Chapter 14: Celebrating Success: Achievements and Milestones of Black Republicans

Welcome to Chapter 14, where we take great pleasure in commemorating and celebrating the remarkable accomplishments and significant milestones of Black Republicans. In this chapter, we pay our utmost respects to trailblazers who have broken barriers, overcame challenges, and left an indelible mark on both our nation and party. Join us as we honor their inspiring stories that have had lasting impacts across politics, community leadership, and entreneurship culture education as they provide hope, inspiration, and an example of perseverance and determination that stands the test of time.

Historic Political Victors:

Black Republicans have left an indelible mark on history through their exceptional political victories, shattering barriers, challenging norms, and forging new paths forward for future generations. From iconic figure Edward Brooke - elected the first African American since Reconstruction to both House of Representatives and Senate from South Carolina respectively - to trailblazer Tim Scott who achieved both office milestones simultaneously - these exceptional individuals have demonstrated how important diversity of leadership is to maintaining a vibrant democracy.

Community Leadership and Advocacy:

Black Republicans have displayed exceptional community leadership and advocacy, dedicating themselves to uplifting marginalized communities while championing important causes through grassroots initiatives and national organizations. Through community development projects and educational reform campaigns, they have actively been part of pushing towards economic empowerment as well as criminal justice reform efforts - their unwavering dedication has played a pivotal role in creating opportunities and making positive contributions that contribute toward change that builds a more inclusive society.

Black Republicans have consistently excelled at business and entrepreneurship, becoming powerful agents of economic expansion and inspiriting others to follow their dreams. From pioneering CEOs to innovative small business owners, their successful entrepreneurial efforts have proven that hard work, perseverance, and adherence to free market principles can result in remarkable achievements that leave an indelible imprint on our economy - creating jobs while stimulating development across industries once thought unreachable by making lasting impactful changes for betterment in America today.

Cultural Influence and Artistic Achievement:

Black Republicans in public view - including artists, entertainers, and cultural icons - have used their platforms to advocate for positive change while challenging societal norms. From musicians and actors, writers to visual artists; all have contributed creative works with diversity of thought that enrich the cultural landscape through unique individuality, opening doors for others while sparking meaningful discussions that inspire future generations of change agents to use their voices positively for change.

Education Advancement:

Education has long been seen as a vehicle to increase empowerment and upward mobility for Black Republicans. Their efforts as educators, policymakers, advocates, and reformers have broken down barriers, promoted innovative reforms and ensured every child received quality instruction - helping those break free of generations-long poverty patterns while fulfilling their dreams.

Legacy and Inspiration:

Black Republicans' achievements and milestones have created a legacy that continues to inspire us today. Their stories stand as testaments of resilience, determination, and unwavering belief in liberty, equality, and individual opportunity principles - reminding us of all that hard work pays off with success being achievable no matter your boundaries and dedication toward values pursuit. Their legacy extends far beyond individual accomplishments to inspire future generations to dream big, overcome challenges, and strive for excellence.

Conclusion:

As we honor and recognize the outstanding accomplishments and significant milestones achieved by Black Republicans who have left an indelible mark on our party and nation. Their successes in politics, community leadership, entrepreneurship, culture, and education serve to motivate us towards setting higher goals, breaking down barriers, and reaching further. Let us honor their legacies by building on their successes, celebrating their victories, learning from their stories, and building on them ourselves to shape a brighter future where diversity, resilience, and the search for success unify all peoples of this society.

Chapter 15: The Road Ahead: Future Challenges and Opportunities for Black Republicans

Welcome to Chapter 15, as we embark on our exploration into the future of Black Republicans. In this chapter, we examine both challenges we might encounter as well as exciting opportunities awaiting us on our political journey - providing a road map that encourages resilience, strategic thinking, and dedication to core values as we navigate an ever-shifting political environment with enthusiasm for progressing our core beliefs forward. As we gaze outward into an optimistic future, we recognize our success depends on meeting challenges head-on while seizing opportunities presented to us along the way.

As Society Evolves:

Black Republicans face the daunting challenge of communicating their principles and policies effectively across multiple audiences. We must work to dismantle misconceptions, break stereotypes and address bias through meaningful dialogue - while simultaneously celebrating diversity within our party and forging connections across communities nationwide to broaden appeal, extend influence, foster an inclusive political landscape, and increase voter turnout among potential constituents.

Building Inclusive Coalitions:

One of our major challenges involves forging inclusive coalitions made up of individuals from diverse backgrounds and ideologies. For Black Republicans, collaboration across communities must be fostered actively so we can find common ground to work toward common goals together. By seeking partnerships, listening to diverse views, and advocating policies that benefit all Americans simultaneously we can bridge political divisions to form more inclusive and united national structures.

Youth Engagement and Mentorship:

Engaging and motivating Black Republicans of today can be both a challenging yet enriching process, so as leaders we cannot afford to overlook either challenge. By mentoring and supporting young Republicans as effective representatives for our principles and providing education programs and mentorship programs that empower young Republicans, as well as providing spaces where young Republicans can voice their ideas, we can ensure our party remains vibrant, innovative, and in tune with modern times.

Policy Innovation and Adaption:

Given today's shifting political environment, Black Republicans must embrace policy innovation and adaptation. By responding proactively to emerging issues like technological advancements, healthcare access, climate change, and others while remaining true to conservative principles we can remain relevant in shaping policy agendas that resonate with a broad electorate. By seeking creative solutions through thought-provoking policy debates as well as adapting our approaches in response to changing national needs we can ensure effective shaping agendas which resonate across multiple voter segments.

Effective Messaging and Communication Strategies:

Crafting compelling messages and employing effective communication strategies are keys to connecting with a diverse electorate. Black Republicans must leverage storytelling, emphasizing personal experiences that resonate across communities. Through platforms like social media, grassroots organizing, and traditional media we can effectively convey our messages, dispel misperceptions about us as Americans, and engage voters in meaningful conversations on America's future - ultimately strengthening democracy itself.

Redefining Republican Identity:

Black Republicans have an unparalleled opportunity to shape and redefine the identity of our party, challenging stereotypes, broadening narratives of conservatism, and pushing policies tailored specifically for our communities. By advocating for an inclusive Republican Party which values diversity, opportunity, and social justice we can attract new supporters while breaking down barriers - creating a powerful political movement that represents all Americans equally.

Conclusion:

Black Republicans face both difficult and rewarding journeys ahead. We can seize this moment to address changing societal landscape, create inclusive coalitions, engage youth groups, embrace policy innovation, refine our messaging and redefine Republican identity together to shape a future where our principles and values flourish while creating positive changes within ourselves, communities and nation we hold dear - ultimately furthering liberty, equality, and opportunity for all. With resilience optimism and commitment toward progress, we will ensure this dream becomes a reality for Americans.

Our journey may have its challenges, yet we stand united in

our collective vision for a brighter future.